ART
DESIGNS TO
COLOR

Illustrated by Lise Herzog and Mary Kilvert
Design and additional illustrations by Emily Beevers

Written by Emily Bone and Hazel Maskell

Arts and Crafts

Arts and Crafts was a style started in the late 19th century by a group of British artists, led by William Morris. It soon spread across Europe, America and Japan. Artists and designers believed that everything – from wallpaper to furniture and pottery – should be made by hand to the highest quality, and be beautifully designed.

Designs often included stylized animal and plant patterns. This pattern has birds among rambling roses.

Artists painted colors from nature – greens, browns and blues, and bright flowers or fruits.

Some artists looked to traditional Asian art for inspiration. This pattern has Japanese Koi carp and blue and purple peonies, a flower popular in China.

Traditional crafts

Arts and Crafts artists believed that everything should be made using traditional methods where possible. They hated the mass-produced, factory-made furniture and pottery that became popular during the 19th century.

This block of wood has been carved with a design. It can be dipped in paint or ink, and then printed onto paper or material.

Woodblocks were used to make wallpaper prints.

Plates and vases were often formed by hand, then painted by an artist.

Everyday objects

Entire houses were built in an Arts and Crafts style, and filled with furniture and accessories to match. Designers wanted their work to be useful as well as beautiful.

This chair has a simple shape, but striking patterns are carved onto its back and embroidered onto the seat.

Orchard tapestry

Hand-stitched tapestries were made to hang on the walls of Arts and Crafts houses. This design has an orchard in the fall with fruit-laden trees, intertwining branches and leaves, and wild animals.

Tapestries like this one were based on medieval designs from hundreds of years earlier. Use greens, blues, oranges and browns to fill in the scene.

Patterned pottery

Pottery was hand-decorated. Artists used patterns inspired by a wide range of different styles, from the Middle Ages to the Far East.

The pattern on this plate is influenced by medieval decoration.

An angel is standing in the middle of a vine of honeysuckle.

The thistle design on this vase is based on patterns from Turkey and Persia (now known as Iran). Color the flowers blue and purple.

This vase is decorated with swans in an elegant style influenced by Japanese art.

On this vase, acorns are growing from highly stylized oak trees.

Wall decoration

Painted tiles or printed wallpaper added decoration to fireplaces and walls.
Some (on the left) were decorated with bold, bright patterns based on Persian and
Turkish art. Others, influenced by medieval art (on the right), were in softer colors.

Time for tea

Tea and coffee pots, cups, jugs and bowls were often made in an Arts and Crafts style. These designs are based on work by a group of American women artists at Newcomb College, Louisiana. They used yellows, blues and greens to create stylish patterns.

The teapot here has patterns made from the seed heads and leaves of iris flowers.

This is a sugar pot, decorated with pansies.

Use greens to fill in the leaves on this jug.

Color these cups green, dark blue and yellow.

Color the flowers on these bowls yellow, pale blue and cream.

The pattern on this coffee pot combines trees and pale pink flowers.

Fabulous fabrics

Arts and Crafts fabrics were often
colored using natural plant dyes.
Many were decorated by hand,
by block-printing or embroidery.

Fabrics like the ones on this page would
have been used for furniture coverings.
Here they are shown on cushions.

Color these with dark blues, rich reds and pale
greens, blues and yellows.

Stained glass

Some designers created stained glass windows based on images
found in old churches. The window below has women
dressed in medieval-style clothing.

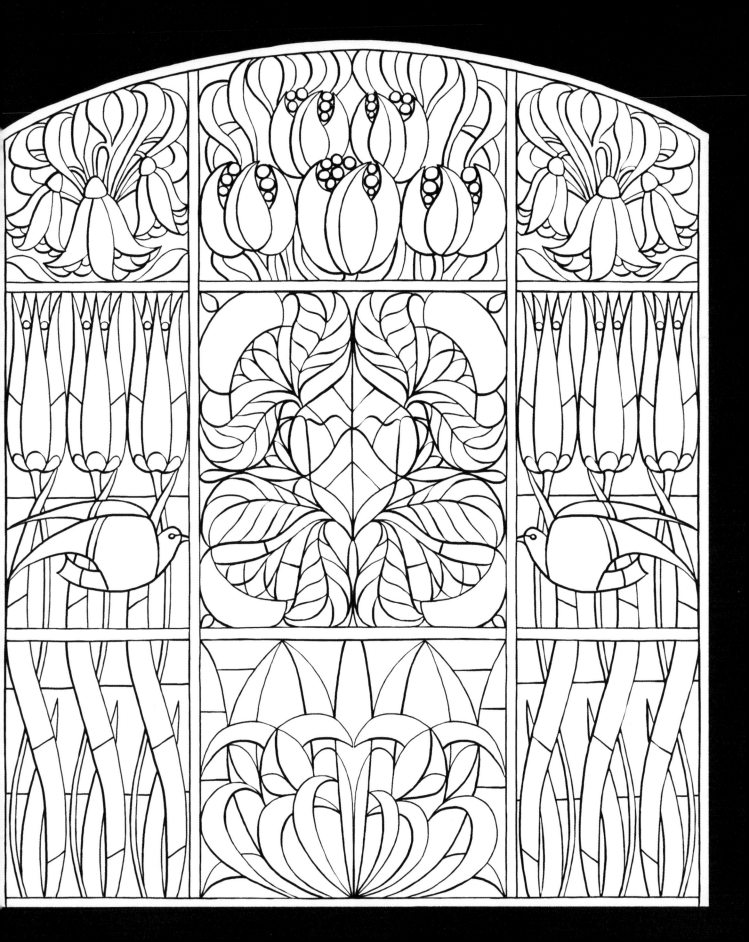

Arts and Crafts fashions

Fashion designers created loose, flowing dresses in rich colors, embroidered with patterns of flowers, leaves, and vines. Many based the shapes and decorations of their creations on medieval styles.

Flowers were popular natural accessories.

This robe is gold with white and pink flowers.

Color this dress green and orange.

Dresses in these styles were famously sold at Liberty's,
a department store in London, which is still open today.

This robe has a turquoise
and pink vine pattern.

Color this
Oriental-style coat
with gold.

Jewelry

Jewelry and other accessories were made of gold, silver or steel. They could be decorated with colorful stones, or with enamel – a type of bright glass fused to the metal.

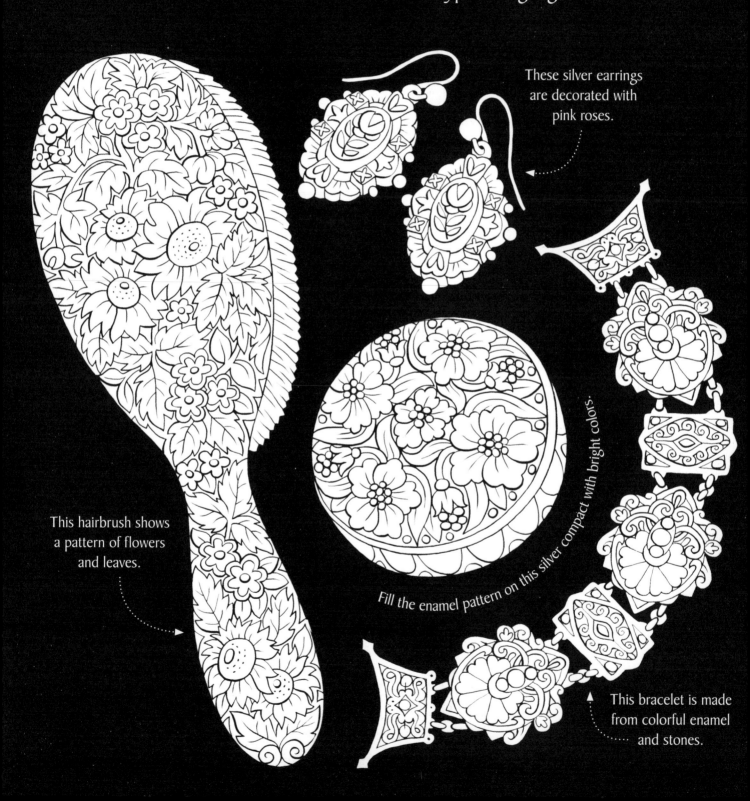

These silver earrings are decorated with pink roses.

This hairbrush shows a pattern of flowers and leaves.

Fill the enamel pattern on this silver compact with bright colors.

This bracelet is made from colorful enamel and stones.

This necklace is studded with diamonds, purple amethysts and pearls, surrounded by clusters of bright green enamel leaves.

This perfume bottle is engraved with a thistle pattern.

This is a silver hair comb. Color the stones with light blues or pinks.

Books and printing

The most sumptuous Arts and Crafts books were bound with ornate leather covers that were dyed, then decorated with gold. The pages were printed with decorative type, influenced by medieval manuscripts.

Myths and folk art

This scene is based on hand-woven tapestries from Scandinavia,
inspired by myths, tales and traditional folk art,
as well as northern European landscapes.

The man on horseback in this scene is a famous 12th-century Norwegian king named King Sigurd. The robes of the dancing figures on the left are modeled after dragonflies. Use rich blues, greens and yellows for the figures, reds and oranges for the flowers, and a dark blue to color the starry sky.

Arts and Crafts patterns

All the patterns on the following pages are based on designs found on Arts and Crafts artifacts – prints, wallpapers, textiles, tiles and pottery.

Usborne Quicklinks

For links to websites where you can find out more about the Arts and Crafts movement and its key figures, including William Morris, Walter Crane, Charles Voysey and many more, and see examples of their work, go to the Usborne Quicklinks website at www.usborne.com/quicklinks and enter the keywords 'Arts and Crafts patterns'. Please follow the internet safety guidelines at the Usborne Quicklinks website. We recommend that children are supervised while using the internet.

Art Nouveau patterns to color

Art Nouveau patterns

Art Nouveau is an ornate design style made up of curved lines and stylized plants and animals. French for 'new art', it became popular in Europe at the end of the 19th century and was very different than existing art and design.

Natural art

Art Nouveau artists and designers were inspired by things in nature. Patterns had bold, simplified flowers on twisting stems and vines. Many patterns featured insects and birds, too.

Soft pastel colors, such as turquoise, purple, pink and pale blue were mixed with gold and black.

Flowers with soft petals and long stems, such as poppies, were popular.

Peacocks and peacock feathers were used in many designs.

Art Nouveau-style butterfly with patterned wings

Vine and leaf patterns were made into decorative borders.

Nouveau fashion

Many fashion designers were influenced by Art Nouveau. Dresses were made in loose shapes, and fabric was printed or embroidered with Art Nouveau patterns.

Accessories were small and delicate. Many were made to look like insects or flowers.

Hats were often decorated with flowers and feathers.

Dragonfly brooch

Evening coat with flower print from 1912

Outside and in

Buildings were designed with decorative windows and doors. Vases, glassware and other everyday objects were made in unusual shapes and painted with patterns.

This Art Nouveau vase has a stand and handles shaped like a climbing vine.

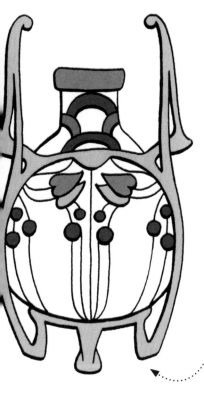

Advertisement art

Advertisements had bold type and striking patterns or figures done in an Art Nouveau style.

This distinctive Art Nouveau-style type is taken from an advertisement for soap.

SAVON

Flower art

Simplified, repeated flowers were popular patterns for textiles and interiors. Artists often painted women surrounded by flowering vines or garlands.

Nouveau in fashion

Fashion designers created elegant gowns, robes and capes printed with Art Nouveau patterns.

This dress and cape have a matching feather pattern.

This dress is decorated with
a pattern that looks a bit
like an Indian vine. Color it
gold, pink and purple.

Turquoise wide-brimmed
hat with gold feathers
and red roses

Nouveau accessories

Accessories decorated with ornate flowers, insects or birds added elegant Nouveau touches to fashionable outfits.

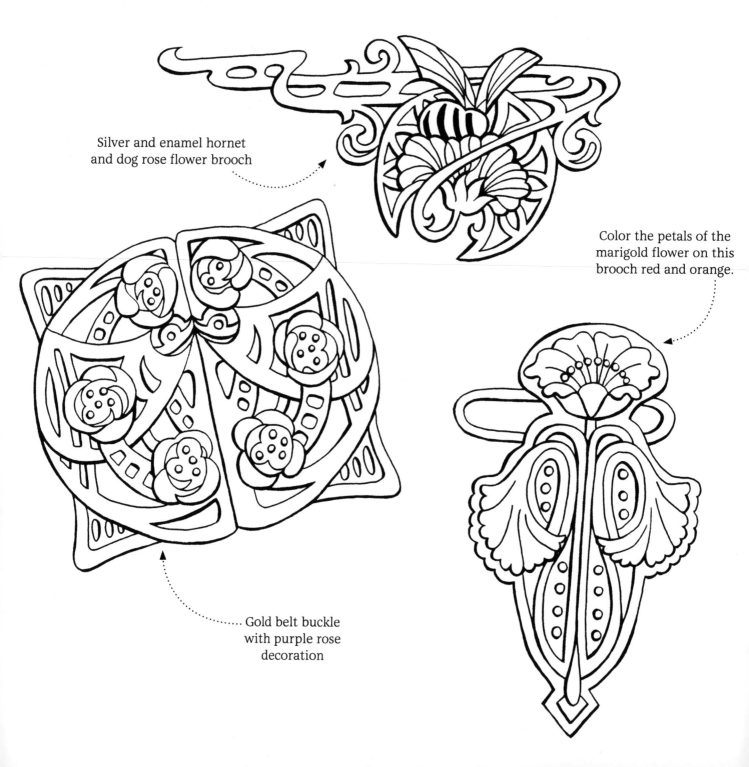

Silver and enamel hornet and dog rose flower brooch

Color the petals of the marigold flower on this brooch red and orange.

Gold belt buckle with purple rose decoration

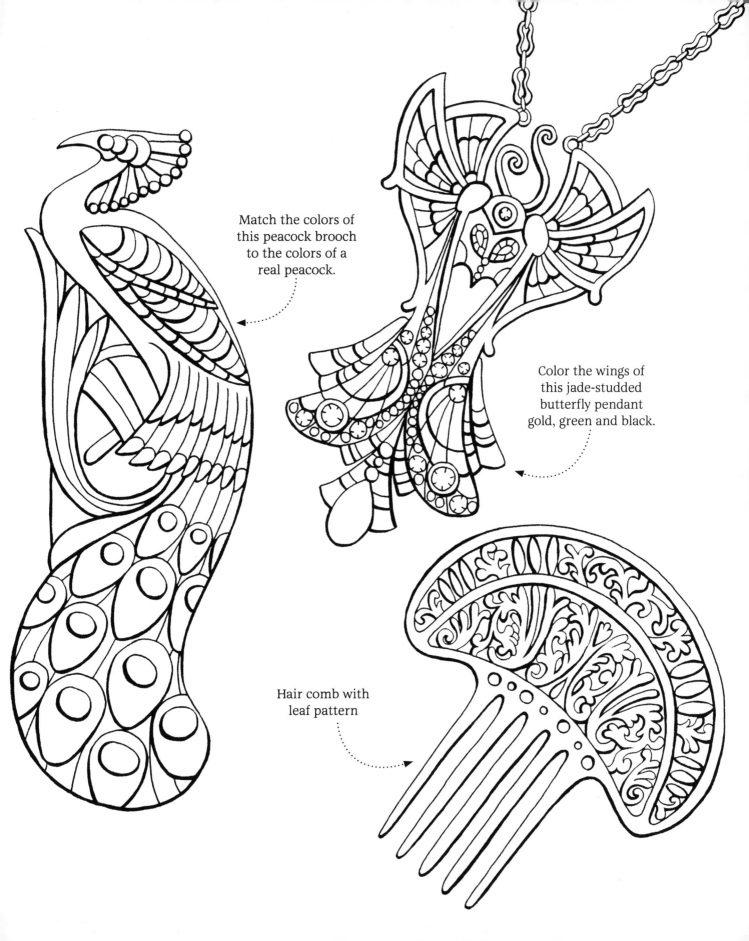

Match the colors of this peacock brooch to the colors of a real peacock.

Color the wings of this jade-studded butterfly pendant gold, green and black.

Hair comb with leaf pattern

Nouveau home

Plates and vases had gently curved outlines and were
decorated with Art Nouveau patterns.

The base and handles
on this vase are
designed to look like
leaves and vines.

This vase is shaped like a
bunch of lily flowers.

Beautiful buildings

Streets in some European cities, such as Paris, Brussels, Budapest and Vienna, were lined with stunning Art Nouveau buildings. They had ornate windows and doors, and highly patterned bricks and tiles.

This door is surrounded
by twisting lines of metal,
called wrought iron.

Glamorous glass

Some Art Nouveau buildings were designed with
beautiful stained glass windows.

Lighting up

Colorful glass lampshades
lit up stylish interiors. Some
designers became known for
their Art Nouveau lamps.

Use bright colors to
fill in these lampshades,
as though the light is
shining through them.

Arty advertisements

Advertisements from the Art Nouveau period were designed in a flat style with patterned borders and bold, distinctive type. These posters are advertising perfume and soap.

CLUB DE DANSE

Clubs commissioned artists to create striking posters promoting shows and star performers.

Nouveau Japanese

Many designers looked to traditional Japanese art for inspiration. These Art Nouveau designs use Japanese clothing, flowers and birds.

The swirling line patterns in both these pictures are designed to look like rippling water.

Art Nouveau patterns

All the patterns on the next few pages are based on Art Nouveau designs taken from fabrics, buildings and interiors.

Usborne Quicklinks

For links to websites where you can find out more about the Art Nouveau movement including key artists and their work, go to the Usborne Quicklinks website at www.usborne.com/quicklinks and enter the keywords 'Art Nouveau patterns'. Please follow the internet safety guidelines at the Usborne Quicklinks website. We recommend that children are supervised while using the internet.

Art Deco
patterns
to
color

Art deco patterns

Art deco is a design style made up of angular and curved shapes that became popular during the 1920s. In the early 20th century, many artists and designers used elements of art deco in their work.

A new style

From art and architecture to fashion and tableware, art deco affected all forms of design.

Flowers, animals and other things from nature were simplified. Art deco patterns had repeated shapes and all kinds of bold, contrasting colors.

Black provided a stark contrast to bright colors.

Flowers, like these poppies, were given simple outlines.

A pattern of flying seagulls

This is a 'sunburst', a popular art deco pattern that looks like rays of sunshine.

Day to day

Art deco vases, tea sets, glasswear and other everyday objects brought deco design into people's homes. Things were made in surprising shapes and were covered in colorful patterns.

This deco vase has a sharply curved outline, and is decorated with a pattern of overlapping semi-circles.

Fashion

Fashion designers were inspired by art deco shapes and patterns. Dresses and overcoats were designed with sharp lines and fabric was printed with art deco patterns. Jewelry was big and bold.

The fringing of this dress from 1925 is cut into a curved pattern.

Bold buildings

Buildings had striking designs too, like this spire from the Chrysler building in New York. It's designed as a sunburst with triangular windows that sparkle when they catch the sunlight.

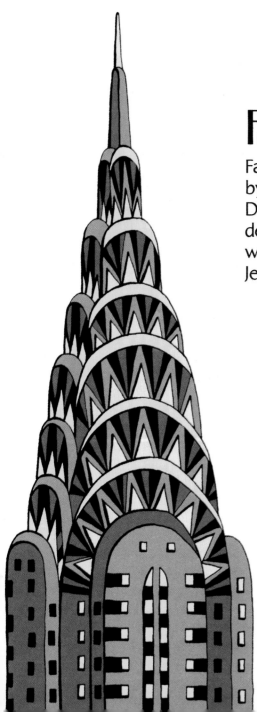

Deco advertisements

Advertisements from the deco period were designed in a flat, yet decorative, style. Pictures like these would have appeared in fashion magazines.

Vacation resorts commissioned artists to create eye-catching posters with bold and distinctive type.

SKI EN CRANS

Fashion show

Fashion designers experimented with simple, clean lines and repeated art deco patterns and colors. Here are some examples of deco-style outfits.

Big, bold flower patterns were popular.

Use alternate bright colors with black to fill in the patterns on this dress.

Art deco parasol

The colors of the stripes on this coat should match the striped hat.

Dressing table

Even small things were given the art deco treatment. You might have found these on a 1920s dressing table.

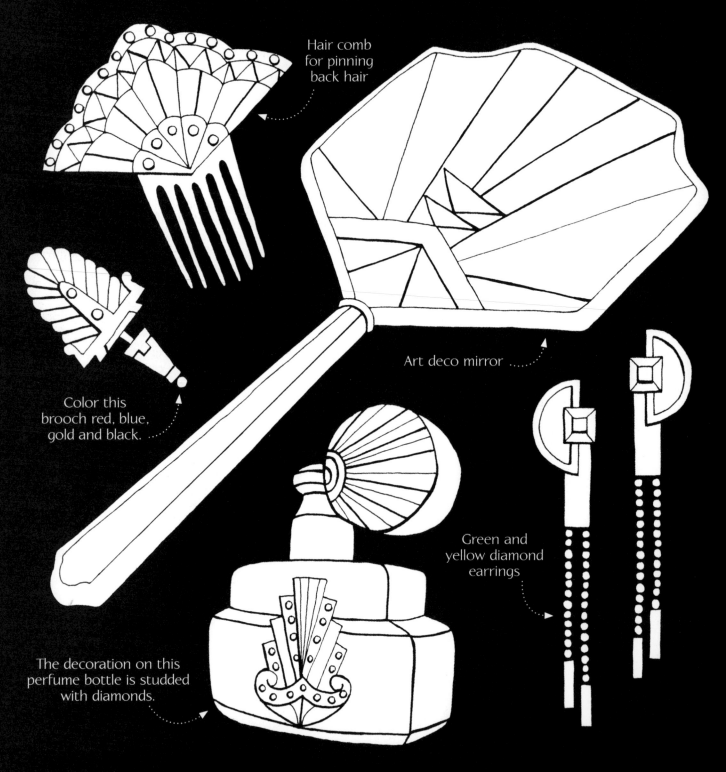

Hair comb for pinning back hair

Art deco mirror ......

Color this brooch red, blue, gold and black. ......

Green and yellow diamond earrings

The decoration on this perfume bottle is studded with diamonds.

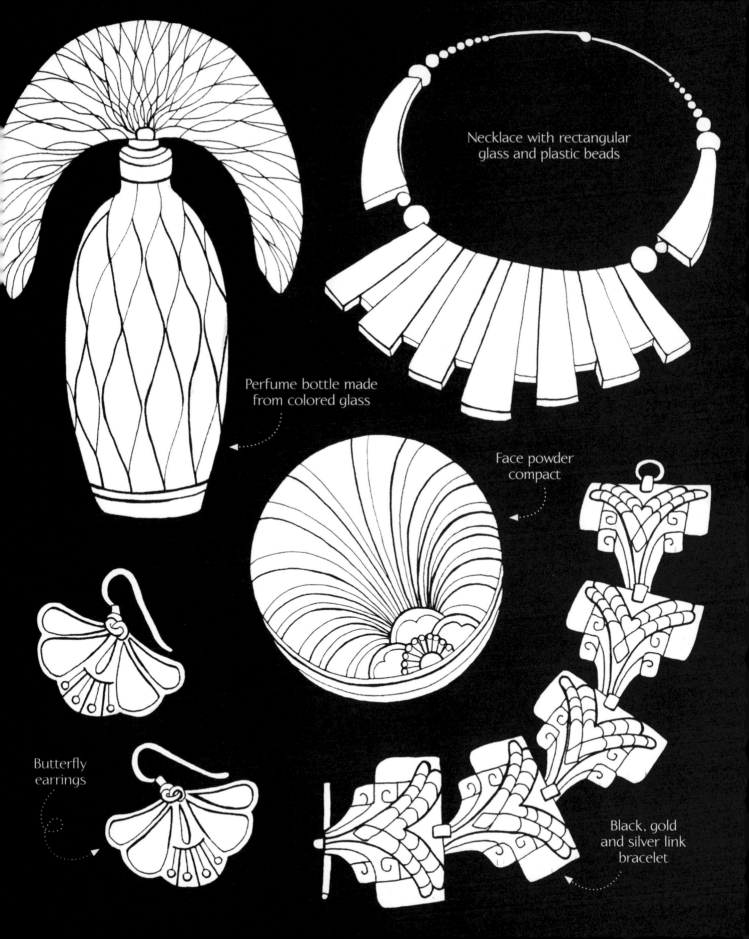

Necklace with rectangular
glass and plastic beads

Perfume bottle made
from colored glass

Face powder
compact

Butterfly
earrings

Black, gold
and silver link
bracelet

Fashionable fans

Fans were fashionable accessories. They were often decorated with striking patterns, like these.

Time for tea

In fashionable tea rooms, people were served afternoon tea in art deco sets. As well as being decorated with patterns, the outlines of cups, pitchers and sugar bowls reflected the curved and angular art deco style. Designers became known for their art deco pottery.

Try to match the rest of the tea set to the colors on this plate.

This milk jug has an interesting mix of different patterns – sunburst and flowers.

These tea cups have sharp, triangular handles.

In the city

The first skyscrapers were built in the 1930s. They had gleaming, deco-style spires. Some buildings had curved walls painted with different patterns.

Glamorous glass

Some art deco buildings were designed with stunning, stained glass windows. This window has a sunburst pattern.

Oriental patterns

Many designers were inspired by patterns used in traditional Asian and African art. Here are art deco versions of ancient Japanese textile designs.

Dazzling art deco costumes and stage designs added
to the spectacle of ballets and musicals.

Art deco patterns

All the patterns on the next few pages are based on art deco designs taken from fabrics, buildings and interiors.

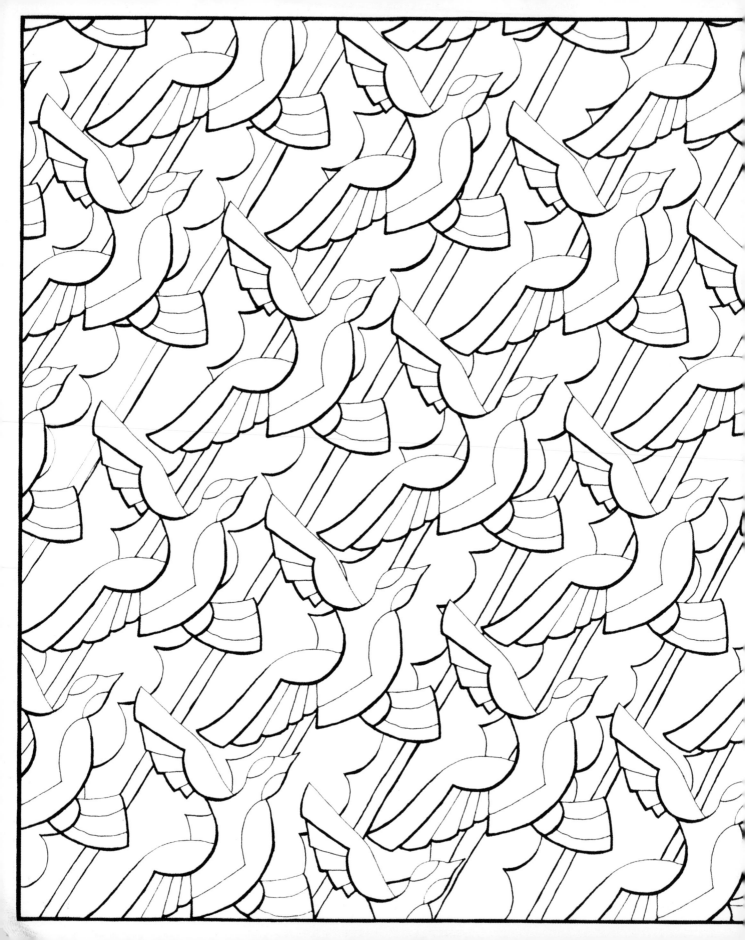

Usborne Quicklinks

For links to websites where you can find out more about Art Deco, go to the Usborne Quicklinks website at www.usborne.com/quicklinks and enter the keywords 'Art Deco patterns'.
Please follow the internet safety guidelines at the Usborne Quicklinks website. We recommend that children are supervised while using the internet.